Merry Christmas to Catherine,

Love,
Lily & Louie

ALPHABEARS

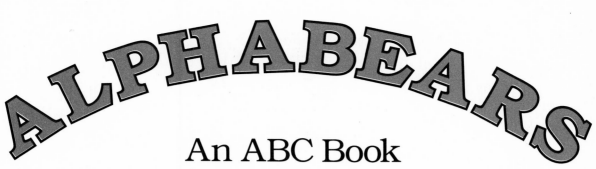

An ABC Book

By Kathleen Hague

Illustrated by Michael Hague

Holt, Rinehart and Winston

NEW YORK

Text copyright © 1984 by Kathleen Hague
Illustrations copyright © 1984 by Michael Hague
All rights reserved, including the right to reproduce
this book or portions thereof in any form.
Published by Holt, Rinehart and Winston,
383 Madison Avenue, New York, New York 10017.
Published simultaneously in Canada by Holt, Rinehart and
Winston of Canada, Limited.

Library of Congress Cataloging in Publication Data

Hague, Kathleen.
Alphabears: an ABC book.

Summary: Introduces a bear for each letter of the
alphabet and describes its special qualities in rhyme.
[1. Alphabet. 2. Bears—Fiction. 3. Stories in
rhyme] I. Hague, Michael, ill. II. Title.
PZ8.3.H1193A   1984   [E]   83-26476
ISBN: 0-03-062543-2

First Edition
Printed in the United States of America
1 3 5 7 9 10 8 6 4 2

Composition: Waldman Graphics, Inc., Pennsauken, New Jersey
Color Separations: Offset Separations Corporation, Turin, Italy
Offset Printing and Binding: Krueger, New Berlin, Wisconsin

Designer: Marc Cheshire
Production Editor: Trent Duffy
Production Manager: Karen Gillis

ISBN 0-03-062543-2

To Devon, who's just like his Pop. —K.H.
To my old teddy bear, Potts. —M.H.

A is for Amanda, a good teddy bear
Who carries sweet apples everywhere.

B is for Byron, who snuggles in bed

Mom tucks him in with a kiss on the head.

C is for Charles, a stuffy old bear

He wears a bow tie and a part in his hair.

D is for Devon, who's just like his pop

Their noses are big and their ears sort of flop.

E is for Elsie, an exploring bear

She went to the jungle because it was there.

F is for Freddie, a big frightful mess

What he has been up to no one can guess.

G is for Gilbert, a gruff grizzly bear
Whenever he growls you'd better beware.

H is for Henry, who loves his hot cakes
With honey and butter like his mom makes.

I is for Ivan, an itchy brown bear

He loves to be scratched—first here, then there.

J is for John, who loves jam and jelly

It's easy to see, just look at his belly.

K is for Kyle, a kite-flying bear

He loves days that are breezy and fair.

L is for Laura, who doesn't like lightning
She thinks that the sound of thunder is frightening.

M is for Marc, a mysterious bear
Whenever you visit, you won't find him there.

N is for Nikki—that's just her nickname

Her real name is Ninny, her mother's to blame.

O is for Ollie, a one-year-old bear

He's just learned to walk, but can't climb a stair.

P is for Pam, who loves a parade

She also likes popcorn and pink lemonade.

Q is for Quimbly, a soft quilted bear
Who was sewn by hand with much love and care.

R is for Robert, who thinks that it's great

To sit by the fire and read until late.

S is for Sarah, a snow-loving bear
Just give her a hat and warm mittens to wear.

T is for Tammy, who wrinkles her nose

When you tickle her tummy, her chin, or her toes.

U is for Ursula, a quite useless bear

Who seems to do nothing but just sit and stare.

V is for Vera, a kind gentle vet

She lovingly takes care of anyone's pet.

Wis for William, the great wonder bear

He wears a white cape and soars through the air.

X is the way that this bear marks his place
So when he returns he can find the same space.

Y is for York, who's a very young bear

To sit at the table he needs a high chair.

Z is for Zak, who says that it is true

That zippers do better than buttons can do.

From Amanda to Zak, the bears are at ease

Because now they can say their A, B, Cs.